Forgive the Body This Failure

Also by Blas Falconer

The Foundling Wheel
A Question of Gravity and Light

Edited Anthologies
The Other Latin@: Writing Against a Singular Identity (co-edited with
Lorraine López)
Mentor and Muse: Essays from Poets to Poets (co-edited with Beth Martinelli
and Helena Mesa)

Forgive the Body This Failure

Blas Falconer

Four Way Books

Tribeca

Library of Congress Cataloging-in-Publication Data

Names: Falconer, Blas, author.
Title: Forgive the body this failure / Blas Falconer.
Description: New York, NY : Four Way Books, [2018]
Identifiers: LCCN 2018003712 | ISBN 9781945588174 (pbk. : alk. paper)
Classification: LCC PS3606.A425 A6 2018 | DDC 811/.6--dc23
LC record available at https://lccn.loc.gov/2018003712
This book is manufactured in the United States of America and printed on acid-free paper.

Four Way Books is a not-for-profit literary press. We are grateful for the assistance
we receive from individual donors, public arts agencies, and private foundations.

This publication is made possible with public funds from the New York State Council on the Arts,
a state agency.

PROUD MEMBER

[clmp]

We are a proud member of the Community of Literary Magazines and Presses.

for Daniel, my dear friend (1972-2014)

for my son

for my mother

for Joseph (again)

Contents

Study of Boy with Flowers

As if for you, he holds
them out, red

blossoms sprouting from
his small fist. You know

this place. A man
climbs a tree, children reach

for the shaking branch,
though more than one has died

with the sweet fruit's
round pit

caught in his throat.
The rooster turns

in its pen. Famous for
nothing, this town,

the ground trashed
with petals, but

the boy is singing.
Open your mouth,

which is his mouth,
and how it all begins.

I

Communion

They open their mouths
because hunger speaks

for the spirit. You know
this by the way they close

their eyes, how they push
the world away, all that

light through the window—
unbearable to watch

as watching two people say
goodbye at the airport is—

almost—the public display
of grief, how they hold

each other in
their private dark, which is

its own brief prayer.

Vigil

While you wait, the body sleeps.
The body wakes. The body will
not eat. The body sips. The body is
hot and cold. The body is
broken. The body is lifted and
set down, again. You can hold
the body. You can kiss the body, but
the body sighs. All day, the body is
failing, the mind failing
to forgive the body for this failure.

*

All day, it's almost over.
All day, the body won't,
the body says,
No,

to the water glass,
but air fills the body

the way light fills
the house at night,
so those outside know
someone is living there.

*

The grunt the body makes
when it moves means

something. The body once
lifted its head in sunlight

without regard to itself,
only what it wanted from

the world, what the body
didn't have, which was

the body's appetite,
but pain insists now

the body lie
still. This is one way

the body is brought back
to itself. Pain is

how much the body wants
to turn away.

*

In every room, the body is
what's missing. Why

wouldn't the world

want the body back, what lived
inside the body gone, too.

You, who tended to the body, what

will you do when all
the bedding has been washed

and folded, what pain

will you tend to, now,
if not yours?

Aubade

Having already looked upon her in the bed
where she slept or did not sleep, now, day
and night, and said all he'd come so far to tell
her, he—the brute, crass and proud—stood
before the large window, his back to them
all, looking out onto the woods and, without
turning, raised his hand to the footsteps
coming toward him, the arm reaching out,
to the mouth about to speak and the words
not yet uttered, to the keys, the watch, the
wallet on the table, and the packed bag at the
door, to the room, the house, the foundation
on which it stood, and to the car idling in
the street, the street itself, to the grass in the
field, and the path, the path leading to the
pond where, once, he watched the beautiful
girls splash in summer, and to the pond, both
the water and the fish inside skimming the
bottom, and to the great maples and the wind
blowing through them, to the neighbors and
theirs and theirs, on and on, stirring, eyes
about to open, to the light spreading on their
faces, the first deep breath of the day and

what joy or misery, he supposed waited for them, as if to say, *Stop, Stop,* to the world, and it would.

Early Morning Task

Matter-of-fact, he told me how
she died, when,

and who was there.
He couldn't talk

long, so many still
to call, and I, who leaned

against the kitchen sink,
head bent, half asleep,

the first. He filled
the pause with more

details, a catch, now
in his voice that grew

until his body gave
in to sobs, the words

no longer words but
the story he

needed to tell.
Once, I heard

my father weep. It was like
a rip, a tear

he kept tearing till
the light poured through.

Event

As a crowd gathered, I saw
the field was fertile—

not the coat
I left on a train

twenty-one years ago
but the same

color. It got cold
fast, dark, and everyone

became a silhouette
of the one

he or she had been
minutes before. We sat

or stood among
the trees to listen.

Each glass in our hands held
a little light.

The water trembled—
I could see

that much—like the first
swell of panic, when

you can't tell where
it's coming from.

Hiking at Dusk

I'm just a boy, you said,
but one day I'll die, too,

and it became a mountainside,
the place your hand

pushed me away. On the plane,
lifting off, landing. Among pines

and strange, iridescent birds.
Come back, you cried

from the window, cars
honking. Combing your hair

after a bath at night, this
is how I love you. *I'm scared*

of the dark, you said.
When you fall asleep, I walk

the house aimlessly, collect
the empty cup, the damp towel

from the bathroom floor,
a bucket of stones, turning off

the lights, one by one.

In absentia,

                              the
shut door, keys

on the hook,

the table wiped
down, the tray

of halved

tablets, the
bowl of soap

and water, the

washcloth, the
hairbrush, hair

in the bristles,

someone
whistling through

an open

window, the sound
of another

hammer

working, wind
blowing over

no one,

the rose
bushes' yellow

blooming all

day, the spot
of light on

the grass, the

grass, the
impression made

there.

Heaven

How will
I get

there? How
will I ever know how

to get
there, my son

asks, sobbing
suddenly, months

after, *if*
you don't let

me see
them die.

II

Apology for My Son Who Stops to Ask About His Mother Once More

The branch, bent to the ground as if under the weight of its own white
    blossom, is

    like a sadness I see
            growing inside you. What can
        I do but tell, again, how

under the fluorescent light, she bent
    over your swaddled body, her face

        pale against her dark brown hair,
yours dark against the pale sheet.

That is your story. This
      is your share

    of the world's grief, what you must carry, and
      which I cannot bear
      for you.

Foundling

She offered what she thought
the small body might

need from hers.
When his cries grew, she held

him to the window where
the houses lined

up in rows, but
his mouth shook, full

of his own voice. *What
do you want?* she asked,

at last, looking into
his face. *What do you*

want? At first,
she didn't know

who she was
speaking to, but when

the boy wailed louder, she
let him.

Lullaby

Sorry, says the balloon
descending, says steam

beading the bathroom
mirror. All

day is this
longing—how

I picked you up
and walked, how

my arms grew
tired. In the darkroom,

the door is framed
in light, but who

you are is
a question no

picture can
answer. When I close

my eyes, I see
your eyes

closing.

Use Your Words

You said bad men waited inside
your mouth, which meant a fire

was catching. We drove toward
a cloud of smoke that rose above

the city. In the mirror, I saw
the wide belt strapped across

your chest, and on the radio,
men stormed the gates

in another country. *I* do
love you, you said, looking out.

The window held the sun
flatly. I held my breath. The brush

had not been cleared in weeks,
and the mountain prepared to burn.

History

"Every moment happens twice: inside and outside,
and they are two different histories." —Zadie Smith

I.

I did not, you insist,
the words garbled by

the dark fruit in that
mouth. Even

Union and
Confederate

soldiers declared
a temporary truce,

Mother, to pick
blackberries, the tea

believed a cure
for dysentery—hands

that killed and
would kill plucked

the same branch
gently.

It makes a good
story, but it's

the story we can't
agree upon

and the field
darkens more

sweetly because we will
not enter it.

2.

The truth is that I called you worse if only to make you stop.
You became a place I once lived and loved but no longer longed for.
Then a friend stopped dancing to say, *I don't know who or when, but
        someone loved you, once.*
And I recalled how you sat on my bed, rubbing my back in the dark,
        singing.

Your mother blamed the sun for her dark complexion but didn't know
        who her father was.
She stopped me, once, in the narrow hall as I made my way in a towel.
Still wet from the shower, I held the knot at my waist.
Above us hung a replica of Goya's *Naked Maja*, and I could see, now, that
        her mouth was moving.
Are you? she asked a second time, her fist rising over my head.

One night, my son woke up and wandered the hall, sobbing.
I picked the child up and rocked him until his body stopped shaking.
My son, who looked like her.

You are a fucking idiot, a stupid faggot, you said,
your meaning made clear through pitch and tone, pace and breath, your
        face pressed close to mine, begging to be hit.

3.

After the pain
is made

public again

we hang on
the line,

your mouth
(open)

mine—

the crooked tooth.
The glass

at your bedside,
the long

stem—if I
imagine it

empty
does this mean

it isn't real?
Buds break

in the California

dark. *Don't go,*
I'd say each night

as you turned
away. *One*

more story. When
will we be

done
with our

unnecessary
grief? Language

can't exhaust
us. We've sung

every
pitiful note.

Orphan

After Nocturnal (Horizon Line), Teresita Fernández, graphite, 2010

I'd come to help settle your own
mother's affairs. On the last night,

we ate where she worked
all her life. *Now that she's gone,*

you said, *I'll never come back.*
Looking out over the dark, you saw

a light in the distance, a boat
crossing the bay, and told

the story of the fisherman
cursed to float adrift

forever. You hadn't thought of it
since you were a child, and held

your hand across the table to show
me how it trembled.

I didn't understand until, alone,
years later, wandering the city where

I was born, I stood before
a black wall, polished to shimmer,

and it looked to me like the sea
at night, hard and endless.

Evening Walk

The conversation I have
with myself all day

is the one we
never finish. I don't want

to think of us
less and less, the field

spreading out
until the moon between the trees

is just another thing
I don't tell you.

Inflection Upon Your First Meeting

I set my son down on the floor, where he wandered about, drowsy and
wordless.

You sat in the old, brown chair, watching him, your grandson, from the
far corner.

He brought you a book about the body, the parts of the body, and you
lifted him into your lap.

We didn't look at each other, we hadn't, but as you read, I recalled how
you would speak sometimes with this tenderness, and how I
wouldn't leave without first kissing you, so each departure felt less
like a betrayal.

You read it together, as he and I had, so many mornings, slowly turning
the pages.

They were familiar and worn, and he pointed to every picture, looking up
to see if you were looking.

III

Metamorphosis

My father's encyclopedia diagramed the transformation stamped on the
    cells of each jellied egg weeks before—how the legs bud, how the
    skin and mouth change in texture and shape, the tail and gills
    absorbed by the body, as the body makes room for the lungs.

When I stood so long one afternoon at the open door of my uncle's
    bedroom, where he slept naked, only a sheet to cover him, this
    man with the same name, the likeness in our faces undeniable,
    though his eyes were blue, I saw the laws with which my own
    body had already been written.

Watching him was like kneeling at the edge of the creek, empty jar in
    hand, as they rose to the surface for air.

Amor Fati

We wrestled in
the basement, drunk,

my head pressed
hard into the coarse,

blue rug, windows dark.
Upstairs,

my mother stood
at the stove. *Soon,*

my body seemed
to say, turning

under you. It was
1986: the fire

at Dupont Plaza, the
Human

Immunodeficiency
Virus, the

Challenger falling in
pieces over

the Atlantic. You
pinned me

there, bent
so close, I thought

we might
kiss, your shirt

stretched by
my long pull,

and I held on
with both fists.

Passing

Our heads full of someone
else's story, we
empty the theater

without words, and shuffling from
one dark to another, wander home,
the plaza dead, the bar

closed, someone crying in
the street. For what? To whom?
No one
knows. The doors

locked, we lie
in bed and dream
a language of
our own.

On Desire

My body was its own
calamity. I locked

the door and stood
in the mirror to

consider what had begun
to change against my will.

This was my father's razor, but
who was my father,

a man? And what
was that? The window looked

on the neighbor's house
where the oldest son

spent afternoons beneath
his car, the drive strewn

with tools, his hands
and shirt smeared with grease.

One day, he called
to me from his garage

where I found him
leaning against the far wall.

Come closer, he said,
his jeans pulled down

to his thighs, and I
didn't but wanted to.

How It Began

Is it a bruise? Is it
the way the light

from the television falls
across her face? A *mis-*

take, she claims. An *ac-*
cident, her lover says.

I sit on the edge
of their bed. *What about*

your call begging me
to come home quick?

As my coach pulled
into the drive, he asked

if I wanted him
to come inside. The first

man I ever loved, how
terrible it seemed. *No,*

I said, which was a lie.
All night, in my room,

all I can hear is
the film they have chosen.

I could not tell you why,

back then, he picked my body up
or how he threw it to

the ground as if it weighed
nothing. How the night was,

years later, imprinted there
still: flashing lights

on the stairs, men circling in
to see, the music's bass

beating through us all.
My knees, my elbows broke

the fall each time, and each time
I stood less, stood less

stunned. Bouncers tossed us out
on the street where I looked into his face.

My junior year, the boy who sat
behind me, day after day, pressed

his fist into my back, a hurt I learned
to welcome, a kind of affection

I deserved. *Let me take you home,*
he said, blood soaking through

my jeans, my shirt. This is how
hate enters the body. His, to crush

what it could not have,
and mine, wanting him to.

To Love

I thought you were
someone. Then I thought

you were someone
else. I'd heard how

you came into the heart
with your great light. How this

greatness opened up
to seem like emptiness

but—.
            How you made

the body a body
again. The story of

you. The story of you
in every mouth. When a fire

swept through the house,
and neighbors gathered on

the lawn, and my mother wept
in back of an ambulance

until the house stood
dark and hollow in

the greater dark, one
man among the men

in their thick yellow suits
crossed the yard to find

me standing on the walk,
alone. In his gloved hands,

he held the small life I'd left
inside to save my own.

Leave-taking

The way someone folds
a shirt into a suitcase
and lifts it from the bed.

The way someone
exits a room and takes
everything with him.

Shutting the door on
a pocket of stillness.
If the curtain or

the pillow sighs, no one
knows. All week
under the mind's prattle.

If we have nothing to give
each other, we have
nothing to give each other.

A man and a woman touched

at night under stairs,
pinball machines ringing, and,
Sundays, he drove her to

the springs of Coamo, the chapel of
San Germán. Had she ever known
happiness? The road
littered with mangos seemed

to go on
forever. She thought,
The people can't eat

them fast enough,
as if she were not
one of those people.

Gesture

You stretched your hand
across the table and

said something I couldn't hear
over the clatter of forks

and plates, the restaurant's
dumb chatter, and

though the body, once
thrown to the ground

bruised and bleeding for
what it wanted, has

a memory of its own,
how policemen laughed

later, the body also speaks
its own language: your

hand—open before me
and the world

as if to say,
I cannot save you—

holds something
like happiness in it.

IV

Valediction

for Daniel

Falling asleep, I asked,
You'll visit, won't you?

>> *We'll toast you're still*
>>> *alive?* But each door

> in the dream opened
>> into the wrong, brightly lit room

>>>> till I forgot what made
>>>> me angry—or was it

afraid?—and recalled, then,
how months before, I sobbed

>>> into the phone. Dear
>> friend, I tried

>>> to thank you after
>> all—for all—

these years. *Yes,* you sighed.
It's as if we said goodbye

before we knew
anyone was leaving.

Radiante

by Olga Albizu, oil on canvas, 1967

like gold leaf,
hammered and

peeling, halo or
cloak hem,

vaulted ceiling, all
things rendered

heavenly, bright—
a gilded chariot

in the ancient tomb
to bear the dead

from darkest night
to—*This*, I said.

A Simple Proof

The crane's long arm
lifts the beam into the air

as men become the hammer
in the hand, the level or

the drill. They build
a shadow in the field.

They build a room
our son at dusk stoops

in the door to look into—
that dark. *I'll miss*

the grass, he says,
closing his eyes, and lets

a stillness hold the frame
of the thought in his mind.

Motherland Elegy

If a box is a room,
let there be a door.

If a door, a window,
a boy in a blue shirt.

He climbs the green
hillside, acres to

be parceled out,
sold. If you hold

the picture of the boy,
you hold the boy,

you hold the ground
where he stands.

The Sweet Air

The road doesn't have
a name, but cane grew,

once, on either side,
and men stood in fields

with blades to fill the trucks
with their hard work.

When mills closed, no one
cut the stalks. To their

surprise, sugar cost
nothing then, and work

grew hard to find.
They walked to shore,

to town, back and forth
all day. Some carried fish

from the pier, fruit
from the country. Everyone

carried something. If
someone stopped, they climbed

the empty bed—to get a ride
was better than to get

where you were going, though
it got you there

faster. At night the road
lay empty. *Coqui-*

coqui. Coqui-
coqui, tree frogs sang

from the field. The field
filled with the song.

There was nothing
human in it.

The Promised Land

They disassembled the bed, emptied drawers, and left what they found no longer necessary or too heavy, or what held a memory they'd rather not carry: the small deaths, for example, buried in the yard.

Driving away, they didn't stop to look, not once, at the city, blinking in the night.

Tired after all these years and hungry for what they couldn't name, they passed the houses, glancing at each other, now, with new tenderness.

Gone was the barn with its rotting roof.

Gone the broken lock.

Gone the overgrowth, the rusted carport, the little ways one person can diminish another.

They'd been warned of earthquakes and traffic, but wouldn't the light be different there?

In the picture, blinds hung lopsided, and a tree stood outside the window.

There were oranges among the leaves, some of them bright, large, and ready to eat.

Foreigner

From the mountain ridge, lights appear
radiant, the sea

indistinguishable from the sky
at night, which must be

the end of the world, a dark no one
can cross. Wordless, you are

the finger pointing to
the highest branch, a plate pushed away,

though the fruit is sweet and soft.
Men spill from the pier

into the bay and find their bodies strong
again. Before long, you can

anticipate the rhythm pouring from
their mouths, even the laughter a kind

of music you move in. One
by one, the sounds give up

their meaning, *wasp* or *moth*
pinned to the picture in your mind,

and your voice joins the song
before you know it's there.

Revolution

after Myrna Báez' *Platanal*, acrylic on canvas, 1974

Plantain trees gather at the edge
of the orchard, clamor for light

in the foreground. They seem to grow
as one, as if they'd fill the field

and the mountains behind them,
leaves large and frayed. We stood

there, once, or someplace like it, so
here we are again, it seems,

years later, branches leaning over
the road, you in your long skirt,

looking out as if to recall something
you meant to do. *My country*, I hear

you say still. But if that's dusk
in the hills, you know what's

coming to the field. You'll stand
among them till there's nothing left

to see. I'll wait beside you, though
I don't know what we're waiting for.

The Window

after Muriel Hasbun's *Only a Shadow,* (Ester IV), gelatin silver print, 1993-1994

behind her makes
it look as though
she is
the source
of light. Or is it
the branch
in the second exposure,
the veil of small,
translucent leaves
over her face?
She is
human in her
simple dress,
who has suffered as
you and I suffer, though
who would dare
imagine what
she's seen in the streets
of Łódź, the fields
of Auschwitz?
Where the fine
branches have all
but disappeared,
white leaves

are floating: the
memory of
some occasion, a
meeting in
spring, perhaps.
They obscure much
of her face, but
we see
her faint smile. We see
that her eyes are closed.

Epithalamium

It became the bluff
and the shallow stream both,

his hand extended, all
the empty bottles lit

beneath the string of lights
in the canopied parking lot.

Please, he begged in jest,
the most intimate gesture since

he wanted almost nothing. This
was not the hand

coming down like so many
loosened stones, I told

myself, and let him
collapse, the hair on his face

against my neck, our shoes
dragging the broken

concrete as we swayed
among coupled guests

to the singular voice that said
something about love

and washed over everyone.

A Love Poem

I fell asleep to the sound of water moving in the dark.

In the morning, the river, what was left of the snow, filled the window in my hotel room, rushing faster than I'd imagined.

To be here, among the foothills, and not there was like wanting, all at once, to hold the same stone in each hand.

And all at once, there was a center where there hadn't been, the way there seems a center in a field where crows roost in winter.

Call it clarity, or the footing a fisherman finds on the bank, whipping his line in the air above his head.

What I wanted was not possible: After the birds have gone, the great nests of leaves and limbs high among leaves and limbs.

He catches the fish he's wanted all day, pulls the hook from its mouth, and lets it go.

Which I must remember and remember to tell you.

*

Study of Boy and Ocean

The boy on the boat holds one foot
        over the water, certain it
will lift him up—

                not to test so much
        as to draw the spirit, housed
in the body, out. When Peter fell

        into the sea, what made
him doubt? *Grace*
                can only enter where

there's a void
                to receive it, says
Weil, *and it*

                is grace which makes
this void: the sun
                        so bright

when you sink, you can't
see where to go,
                and going down

                becomes another way.

81

Notes

"Apology for My Son Who Asks About His Mother Once More": With special thanks to Jenny Factor, whose words and understanding led me to my own.

"History": The epigraph is from Zadie Smith's *White Teeth*.

"Revolution": When considering Myrna Báez's painting "Platanal," E. Carmen Ramos explains, "When Puerto Rico was a Spanish colony, artists like Francisco Oller depicted the plantain as both a key accoutrement to the *jibaro* [rural peasant] and a metaphor for the island's independent cultural identity." (*Our America: The Latino Presence in American Art.*)

"Study of Boy and Ocean": This quote comes from Simone Weil's *Gravity and Grace*.

Acknowledgments

Some of these poems or versions of them have previously appeared in the following publications:

Alaska Quarterly Review, Bloom, Borderlands and Crossroads: Writing the Motherland, Crab Orchard Review, Dialogist, Diode, Entropy, Harvard Review Online, *MiPoesia, Miramar, Poetry, Poetry Daily, Poetry Northwest, Prairie Schooner, Puerto del Sol, Redivider, Southern Indiana Review, Taos Journal of Poetry and Art, Terrain, Verse Daily, Witness, Written Here: The Community of Writers Poetry Review.*

For their guidance, I want to thank Kazim Ali, Vandana Khanna, Maria Melendez, and Helena Mesa. Also, for their support, my sincere gratitude to Francisco Aragón, Chris Burawa, Victoria Chang, Steven Cordova, Amy Davis, Stephanie Dugger, Rigoberto González, Ilya Kaminsky, David Keplinger, Lorraine López, Mary Szybist, Susan Wallace, Martha Rhodes, Ryan Murphy, and everyone at Four Way Books.

Blas Falconer is the author of *The Foundling Wheel* and *A Question of Gravity and Light* as well as the co-editor of two anthologies, *Mentor and Muse: Essays from Poets to Poets* and *The Other Latin@: Writing Against a Singular Identity*. The recipient of a poetry fellowship from the National Endowment for the Arts and a Maureen Egen Writers Exchange Award from *Poets and Writers*, he teaches in Murray State University's low-residency MFA program and is a poetry editor at *The Los Angeles Review*.

Publication of this book was made possible by grants and donations. We are also grateful to those individuals who participated in our 2017 Build a Book Program. They are:

Anonymous (6), Evan Archer, Sally Ball, Vincent Bell, Jan Bender-Zanoni, Zeke Berman, Kristina Bicher, Laurel Blossom, Carol Blum, Betsy Bonner, Mary Brancaccio, Lee Briccetti, Deirdre Brill, Anthony Cappo, Carla & Steven Carlson, Caroline Carlson, Stephanie Chang, Tina Chang, Liza Charlesworth, Paula Colangelo, Maxwell Dana, Machi Davis, Marjorie Deninger, Emily Flitter, Lukas Fauset, Monica Ferrell, Jennifer Franklin, Helen Fremont & Donna Thagard, Robert Fuentes & Martha Webster, Chuck Gillett, Dorothy Goldman, Dr. Lauri Grossman, Naomi Guttman & Jonathan Mead, Steven Haas, Mary & John Heilner, Hermann Hesse, Deming Holleran, Nathaniel Hutner, Janet Jackson, Christopher Kempf, David Lee, Jen Levitt, Howard Levy, Owen Lewis, Paul Lisicky, Sara London & Dean Albarelli, David Long, Katie Longofono, Cynthia Lowen, Ralph & Mary Ann Lowen, Donna Masini, Louise Mathias, Catherine McArthur, Nathan McClain, Victoria McCoy, Gregory McDonald, Britt Melewski, Kamilah Moon, Carolyn Murdoch, Rebecca & Daniel Okrent, Tracey Orick, Zachary Pace, Gregory Pardlo, Allyson Paty, Veronica Patterson, Marcia & Chris Pelletiere, Maya Pindyck, Taylor Pitts, Eileen Pollack, Barbara Preminger, Kevin Prufer, Vinode Ramgopal, Martha Rhodes, Peter & Jill Schireson, Roni & Richard Schotter, Andrew Seligsohn, Soraya Shalforoosh, Peggy Shinner, James Snyder & Krista Fragos, Alice St. Claire-Long, Megan Staffel, Robin Taylor, Marjorie & Lew Tesser, Boris Thomas, Judith Thurman, Susan Walton, Calvin Wei, Abby Wender, Bill Wenthe, Allison Benis White, Elizabeth Whittlesey, Hao Wu, Monica Youn, and Leah Zander.